LEARN ABOUT VALUES

FORGIVENESS

by Cynthia A. Klingel

Published in the United States of America by The Child's World®
1980 Lookout Drive • Mankato, MN 56003-1705 • 800-599-READ • www.childsworld.com

The Child's World®: Mary Berendes, Publishing Director; Katherine Stevenson, Editor
The Design Lab: Kathy Petelinsek, Art Director; Julia Goozen, Design and Page Production

Photo Credits: © Bryan Allen/Corbis: 19; © David M. Budd Photography: 5, 8, 11, 15, 17, 21; © Grace/zefa/Corbis: cover; © Jim Craigmyle/Corbis: 7; © John Henley/Corbis: 13

Library of Congress Cataloging-in-Publication Data
Klingel, Cynthia Fitterer.
 Forgiveness / by Cynthia A. Klingel.
   p. cm. — (Learn about values)
 ISBN 978-1-59296-668-4 ISBN 1-59296-668-3 (library bound : alk. paper)
 1. Forgiveness—Juvenile literature. 2. Values—Juvenile literature. I. Title. II. Series.
 BJ1476.K58 2006
 158.2—dc22   2006000971

CONTENTS

What Is Forgiveness?

Sometimes people do things that make you feel angry. Sometimes they say or do things that hurt your feelings. Forgiveness means letting go of hurt feelings. When you forgive people, you stop being angry at them. You **accept** their mistakes.

How can we show forgiveness?

5

Forgiveness at School

Imagine that you just got a new book. You cannot wait to read it! You bring it to school to read during library time. Your friend borrows the book. But she forgets to give it back. When she remembers, she says she is sorry. You show forgiveness by not staying mad. You show forgiveness by saying, "That's OK."

We can show forgiveness by not staying angry.

The Teasers

Have you ever been **teased**? Teasing can make people mad. It can hurt their feelings. Imagine that some kids are teasing you. They are making fun of something you did or said. One of your friends starts teasing you, too. Later she says she is sorry. You show forgiveness by not staying angry at her.

Sometimes people forget that teasing can hurt. They might be sorry later.

Feeling Disappointed

You feel good when your parents come to your hockey games. You want them to see you win. But what if your team loses? Maybe other kids on the team made lots of mistakes. You feel **disappointed** that you lost. You might feel angry at the other kids. But you show forgiveness by not getting upset. You understand that nobody wins every time.

Everybody loses sometimes. Maybe your team will win next time!

Mistakes Happen

Your teacher is getting ready for a school party. Some kids cause trouble by playing with the food. Your teacher thinks you were one of them. She is angry and scolds you. You feel hurt. You know you did not do anything wrong. Soon your teacher finds out what really happened. You show forgiveness by not being angry at her. You understand that even teachers can make mistakes.

Anyone can make a mistake!

13

Letting Go of
Bad Feelings

You draw a beautiful chalk picture on the sidewalk. You want to show your mom. You go inside to get her. Your neighbor is watering her yard. She washes off the picture with her hose. You are angry and sad. But you understand that the neighbor made a mistake. She did not know you wanted to keep the picture. You show forgiveness by letting go of your anger and sadness.

Most people do not hurt our feelings on purpose.

15

Brothers and Sisters Need Forgiveness, Too

Maybe your brother likes to pick on you. He grabs your **favorite** toy and takes it outside. But he forgets to bring it back in! That night, it rains. Your toy gets all wet and muddy. Your brother feels bad. He did not mean to ruin the toy. He tells you he is sorry. You forgive him.

Sometimes forgiving people can be hard!

17

Forgiving Yourself

You are visiting your grandpa's house. You reach for a cookie and knock a vase off the table. You feel really bad! You would never do something like that on purpose. But this was an **accident**. You tell your grandpa you are sorry. He understands that it was an accident. He forgives you. And you forgive yourself. You will be more careful next time!

Accidents can help us learn to be more careful.

Forgiveness Is Not Always Easy!

It can be hard to forgive people. You might feel angry or sad or disappointed. Sometimes it is hard to let go of those feelings. But when you do, you feel better. You help the other person feel better, too. Forgiveness helps people get along.

Forgiveness helps people get rid of bad feelings.

glossary

accept
When you accept something, you understand that it cannot be changed.

accident
An accident is something that happens—but not on purpose.

disappointed
Feeling disappointed is feeling unhappy that something you wished for did not happen.

favorite
When you like something best, it is your favorite.

teased
When you are teased, someone makes fun of you.

books

Enright, Robert D. *Rising Above the Storm Clouds: What It's Like to Forgive.* Washington, DC: Magination Press, 2003.

Strazzabosco, Jeanne. *Learning about Forgiveness from the Life of Nelson Mandela.* New York: Powerkids Press, 1997.

Walsh, Sheila. *Einstein's Enormous Error: A Story about Forgiving Others.* Nashville, TN: Tommy Nelson, 2003.

web sites

Visit our Web page for links about character education and values: *http://www.childsworld.com/links*

Note to parents, teachers, and librarians:
We routinely check our Web links to make sure they're safe, active sites—so encourage your readers to check them out!

index

about the author

Cynthia A. Klingel is Director of Curriculum and Instruction for a school district in Minnesota. She enjoys reading, writing, gardening, traveling, and spending time with friends and family.